I Feel...

ANGRY

Words and pictures by

DJ Corchin

sourcebooks
eXplore

Sometimes I feel **angry**

and **throw** toys in the air,

or I **roll** on the ground,

or **hide** under a chair.

I might **snarl** and **growl**

like a **big** grizzly bear,

or put my hands on my head...

Now I have **crazy** hair.

Sometimes I'm so **furious**
'cause I want to go play,

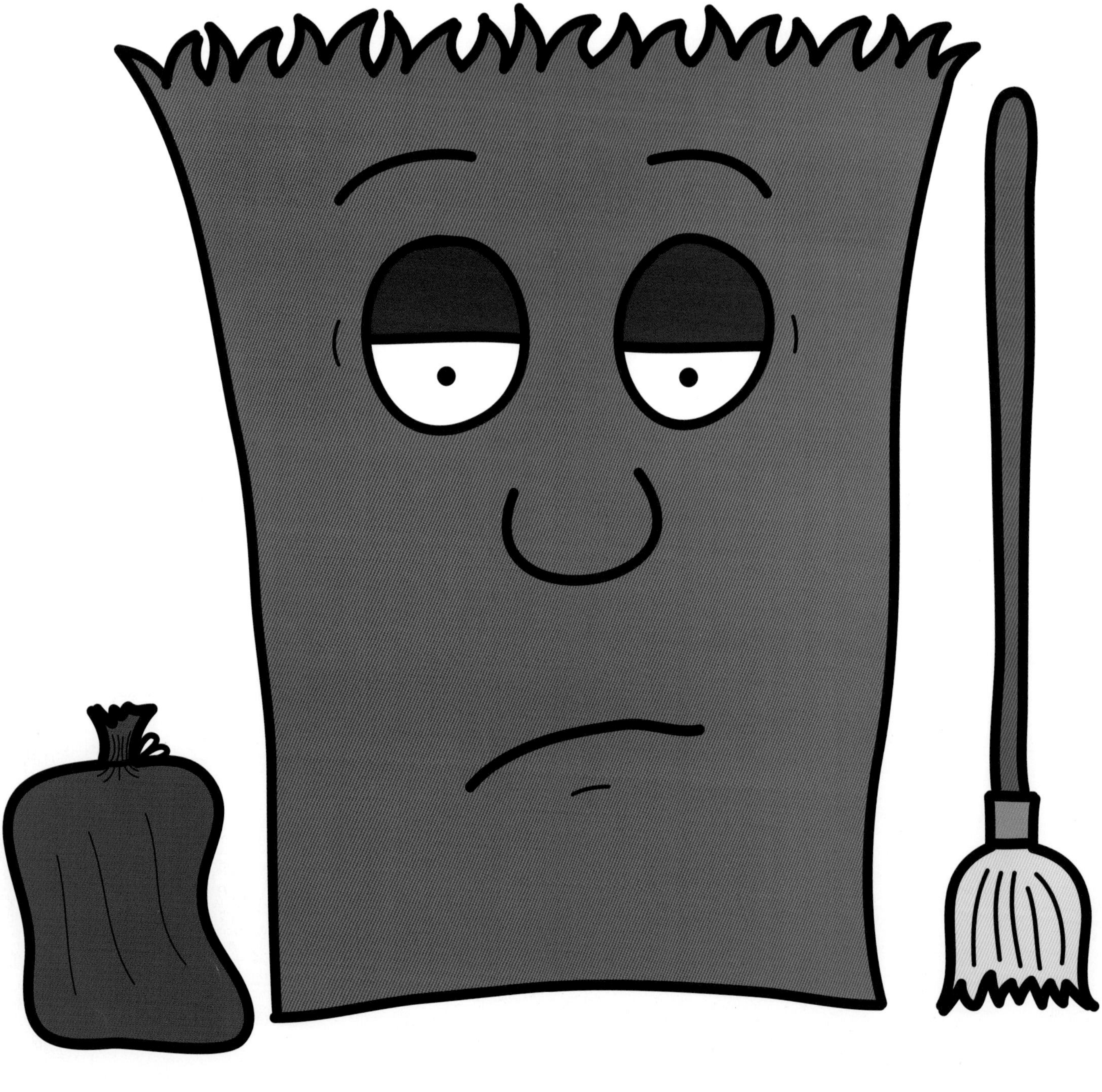

but I'm told to go **clean**

the **fantastic** mess I made.

No candy for breakfast

and no chocolate buffet.

I don't like my choices.
I'm told to **behave**.

Sometimes I'm so **mad** that I turn really red.

There are so many things going on in my **head**,

they come out all wrong
and I **regret** what I said.

So I get even **angrier**
and pound on my bed.

It's so hard to **calm** down,
so I yell and I scream.

I'm just looking for ways to blow off some **steam**.

I might go for a **run**

or get **lost** in a book.

I might **write** down my thoughts

in my thought-**writing** nook.

I could **call** up a friend and invite them to **talk**.

I could **share** how I **feel**
while we go for a walk.

And while we mosey along,
my **temper** subsides,

'cause I think of **kind** things
when I feel **angry** inside.

I Feel...
ANGRY

I get so ANGRY! How do I calm down?

Sometimes you can get angry. Sometimes you can get REALLY angry. It's something everyone feels at times. But when you're angry, it can be hard to say what you really feel or make the best decisions. It's important that you have tools and activities to help you calm down. Here are some suggestions to get started that might work for you.

Create a Thought-Writing Nook

When you're feeling angry, it's important to have a place to think about your emotions. Writing about them is a great way to feel better!

1. Find a corner or space in your home that is quiet and has some light, possibly by a window or near a good lamp.

2. Hang some pictures around your new nook that remind you of calm and happy things.

3. Add a collection of paper, pens, notebooks, markers, or any other writing tools you like.

4. You can add a basket of some of your favorite books that spark your imagination.

5. When you're feeling angry, use this space as a place to go and write down your thoughts. You can even share your thoughts with a caring adult later if you would like.

I Feel... Calm Box

Let's create a box full of things to help you calm down for when you get angry!

1. Find a box big enough to fit a basketball in.

2. On the top or side, label it "I Feel... Calm."

3. Decorate it however you want. You can draw calm and happy faces on the sides or get creative with designs.

4. Fill the box with items and activities that help YOU calm down. Here are some suggestions:

A sand or liquid timer, like an hourglass

A stuffed animal or special object you like to hold

This book!

A squishy ball

A small notebook and pencil

Homemade lavender-scented play dough

The next time you feel angry, sit in a quiet place and open your Feel... Calm Box. You can use the sand timer to give yourself a guided amount of time for an activity. For example, hold your stuffed animal and breathe deeply for as long as it takes the sand to run out of the timer.

My Angry Ally

When you're not feeling angry, find someone to be an Angry Ally to help you through the next time you are feeling angry. You can have more than one!

1. Ask a friend, family member, or caring adult if they would be your Angry Ally. When you're feeling angry, you can reach out to them to communicate to for help.

2. You can call them.

3. You can video chat with them.

4. If they're not available, you can write them an email or letter to mail.

5. You can write in a journal and share it with them from time to time.

6. You can ask them questions about how you're feeling and talk about it.

7. You can simply take a walk together and enjoy each other's company.

It's always OK to ask for help—and nobody ever needs to feel angry alone!

Angry and Wonderful

It's important to focus other thoughts besides just the negative ones. You can find a balance with positive, wonderful thoughts.

1. Grab a piece of plain paper and draw a giant T on it to create two columns.

2. At the top of one column, write the title "ANGRY."

3. At the top of the second column, write the title "WONDERFUL."

4. When you're feeling angry, start writing a list in the ANGRY column of things that are making you feel this way.

5. Then for each thing you list in the angry column, challenge yourself to write another thing in the WONDERFUL column that makes your feel happy or joyous.

Exercise it out!

Sometimes exercising our bodies can help us relax our minds.

1. In your room, do ten jumping jacks, ten push-ups, and ten lunges (or as many as you can comfortably do).

2. You can use your favorite exercise app or videos to follow along for a workout.

3. You can ask to go for a walk or a run with your Angry Ally.

4. You can clean up a really messy room in your house to get your heart pumping.

5. You can go play a sport outside either with a group of friends or by yourself.

It is ALWAYS OK to ask someone for help when you are feeling bad.

The I Feel... Children's Series is a resource created to assist in discussions about emotional awareness.

Please seek the help of a trained mental healthcare professional and start a discussion today.

To Kathy

Published by Sourcebooks eXplore, an imprint of Sourcebooks Kids
P.O. Box 4410, Naperville, Illinois 60567–4410
(630) 961-3900
sourcebookskids.com

Originally published in 2017 in the United States of America by The phazelFOZ Company, LLC.

Library of Congress Cataloging-in-Publication Data is on file with the publisher.

Source of Production: 1010 Printing Asia Limited, North Point, Hong Kong, China
Date of Production: December 2020
Run Number: 5019821

Printed and bound in China.
OGP 10 9 8 7 6 5 4 3 2 1